Introduction

When I first began to put together this book, I
did so from a mind frame that what I wanted to
share were lessons I had learned, and though
not perfect in practice, I was doing OK on my
journey as a follower of Christ. The last couple
of months, God has been calling me out on how
huge of a gap there was between how I saw
myself as a Christian and how I actually
practiced my walk with Jesus. As He revealed to
me just how far I had fallen short of where I
thought I was, my first thoughts were to put this
project on hold and get myself back on track.

But the reality is that what is in these pages is
what I need to revisit in His Word over and over.
Growing up in church and on the mission field, I
always wondered if I would learn everything
there is in the Bible, and if so, what then. Now,
my life a little past the half decade mark, I wish I
could go back and let my young me know that
there is no way I could ever learn everything

there is to learn in God's word. And, I would also warn myself how easy it will be to forget what I learned, that I would need to relearn it over and over and finally, that learning something was not the same as living it. It is in my actions and behaviors that I demonstrate that I believe what I have learned.

The thoughts shared in these pages are based on observations made over the course of my life living in different corners of the world. I grew up the son of missionaries who ministered in Africa, Asia and Europe. After college, my wife and I continued working overseas, as well as in the United States. In all these travels, I have seen many facets that make human beings both unique and similar. I have been blessed to experience a wide variety of cultures and world views. In all of these experiences, what stands out most is how much life around us shapes how we interpret the Scriptures through our thoughts and actions.

Here is an example. A colleague in Guinea, West Africa shared about a cultural difference in understanding that came from a Bible class he was teaching to church leadership. The topic was telling the truth. In the Western culture, truth is that which is fact or reality. In the local Guinean culture, truth is that which makes you or your family look good. Facts and reality are not as important as protecting personal and family image. The concept of truth from the Western culture was so alien that the church leaders felt that if Jesus had been raised in their culture, He would see truth as they did. In their opinion, He would lie (according to our definition) in order to protect His image or His family's reputation.

Experiences like this have led me to thinking about how I was taught about faith, my Christian growth process and how to interpret what God is trying to teach me through His Word. It also has encouraged me to look at what I have put between me and what God is trying to work out in my life. And I am a slow learner; much slower than I originally thought. Thankfully, God loves the slowest learner as much as He loves the fastest.

The other good news is that God has given me a lifetime to learn. It may be a lifetime that has only a few more months or it may have a few more decades. The length of time isn't what is important; it is in never stopping trying to learn and live His Word.

Another thing I learned growing up in different cultures is that language is differs according to the culture. I am not talking about the differences between say English and Chinese. What I mean is how the words we use reflect our culture, our family, our worldview. Even when words are translated easily from one language to another, the meaning of that word can carry a different weight or a different insight. Also, there are many times in all languages where an original word has more meanings than the word used in the English translation. Therefore, I have found it helpful to find a good resource that would bridge this linguistic gap.

Throughout this book, Strong's will be referenced. By this, I mean <u>Strong's Exhaustive Concordance of the Bible</u> by James Strong. This reference work, first published in 1890 is an exhaustive cross-reference of every word in the Bible back to the original Hebrew or Greek. The word usage is based on the King James Version. I have found this reference work to be very useful in bridging the afore mentioned linguistic gap when I am trying to figure out what the original author was trying to say.

And finally, I share this quote

I know about the despair of overcoming chronic temptation. It is not serious, provided self-offended petulance annoyance at breaking records, impatience, etc. don't get the upper hand. No amount of falls will really end us if we keep on picking ourselves up each time. We shall be very muddy and tattered children by the time we reach home. But the bathrooms are all ready, the towels put out, and clean clothes in the airing cupboard. The only fatal thing is to lose one's temper and give it up. It is when we notice the dirt that God is most present in us; it is the very sign of His presence. (C.S. Lewis, *Letters* 1942).

C.S. Lewis penned this to a friend as an encouragement in his Christian walk. It is an observation of his that I find personally very comforting. It lets me know that I am not the only one who finds living the victorious Christian life a struggle. It also reminds me that God is waiting for me each time I reach up to Him, asking for His hand to pull me up out of the mud, yet again.

I pray this will be helpful in your journey.

Just Because I Believe It...

"... you will know the truth and the truth will set you free"[1]In John 8, beginning in verse 31, Jesus begins a discussion with the Jews around Him about true freedom. The people with whom He is talking grow upset at the topic because they think Jesus is implying they are slaves. They protest they are the sons of Abraham; they have never been slaves of anyone. It is important to keep in mind He is not talking to Jewish religious leaders who oppose Him. He is saying this to people who believe in Him (v.31). So, this is not a hostile audience, at least when the conversation begins. But this opening exchange of opinions highlights the challenges Jesus faced then, and that you and I face today, in sharing what we believe.

This challenge is that everyone has his or her own personal way of looking at the same information. How we look at things is rooted in our life experiences, our hopes, our disappointments. These are what influence one

---

[1] John 8.32 New English Translation

person to see a glass as half empty while someone else sees the glass as half full. In this passage from John 8, there is one word in the original Greek that shows Jesus and the people to whom He was talking with were looking at the same glass through different lenses. The lens, or word, in this case is the word "free". And, to understand the two different lenses, we have to go back to that original Greek.

When Jesus says the truth will set them free, the Greek word for free He uses is "*eleuthroo*" (Strong's 1659). What His followers hear is "*eleuthros*" (Strong's 1658). *Eleuthroo* means a freedom from sin. *Eleuthros* means a freedom from physical bondage, to be freed from being a slave. Both mean to be free; they differ in what you are free from. The difference is an "o" vs. an "s" at the end of the word. While I don't have any proof, I don't believe Jesus mumbled. What I believed happened was that what Jesus said was filtered through how His followers saw Him and themselves.

They appreciated His teachings; they thrilled at His miracles. He had authority. He challenged the stuffy Pharisees. He acted like the prophets of old, the ones whose stories they heard repeatedly as they grew up. These stories were a part of their life experience, their hopes, their disappointments. They had the life experience of being under Roman rule. They carried the disappointment of their nation that had long ago lost the glory of David and Solomon. They carried the hope of one day being their own country again, free from the rule of Rome, led by the Messiah promised so long ago. The more they hung around Jesus, the more He seemed to be that promise. So, when Jesus said *"eleuthoo"* they all heard *"eleuthros"*. And so began a discussion that ended with those who had believed in Him ready to stone Him[2]. Why did it go so wrong?

It went wrong because the people were so dedicated to their experiences, their hopes and their disappointments they could not hear the truth Jesus was trying to share. Jesus points this out, "Why don't you understand what I am saying? It's because you cannot accept (or hear)

---

[2] John 8:59

my teaching.[3]" He was talking freedom from
spiritual bondage; they were hearing freedom
from Roman bondage. Jesus knew both what He
was talking about as well as what they were
hearing. All the way through the passage, until
the end of John 8, He kept trying to point the
conversation from freedom from Rome to
freedom from sin. They, on the other hand,
couldn't free themselves to see beyond their
own view, their own hope of freedom, their
desire to be their own nation. The conversation
did not end well.

This exchange is critical for you and me to
understand as we share our faith, our beliefs.
Let's begin with this difficult, but basic
supposition – at a certain level, God left His
Word open to disbelief. He left enough gaps
that we would have to accept some of what is
written in His Word without ever being able to
show irrefutable proof. We have to accept on
faith things we cannot fully explain or prove.
"Now faith is being sure of what we hope for,
being convinced of what we do not see.[4]"

---

[3] John 8.43
[4] Heb. 11.1

I know what many of you are saying, "The Bible is God's word. It is true. I know it is!"I'm not arguing with you. What I will ask is this, "What convinced you it was true?" For some, you may have had a direct encounter with Jesus. The mother of some Cambodian friends of mine came to Christ in the jungle running for her life. One night, in a dream, Jesus came to her and let her know He was taking care of her children. When she finally was reunited with her children, they worked it out that her dream happened about the same time as the children prayed to accept Christ.

For others, nothing else made sense. Charles Colson was the Senior Counsel to President Nixon and one of the Watergate Seven. He went to prison for his efforts to cover-up crimes he and others close to President Nixon committed in efforts to win the 1972 presidential election. He recalls that once it was beyond anyone's doubt they would be caught, tried, convicted and sent to jail, these powerful men were tripping over themselves to confess their crimes. He compared these men to the apostles. All but one would die for the message

of Jesus and the one that lived died in exile.
Their conviction to hold to their "story" even in
death convinced him the message of God's
word was real.

C.S. Lewis set out to prove God didn't exist. He
found the opposite. A Buddhist priestess in a
refugee camp in Thailand finally stopped
resisting God's message of love when the lady in
the hospital bed next to her died with a smile
on her face. Ravi Zacharias found God's love in
an unsuccessful suicide attempt. Others have
watched lives change, transform as they
embraced the Gospel of Jesus. But, while there
are themes that run through accepting the truth
of Christ, of being *eleuthroo*, there is no formula
for convincing them that can be repeated, no "3
Easy Steps to Converting Someone to Christ".

And, before you can begin a conversation about
faith, you have to understand why you believe.
What made Christ real to you? What allowed
you to be *eleuthroo*? Once you know why you
believe, you have to hold that loosely. You hold
it loosely because you know it will be
questioned, challenged. If you let the

conversation become a debate about the rightness of your point of view, it will probably degrade into a contest between you and the person to whom you are trying to show the love of Christ. It becomes you against them and Christ is no longer the focus.

Holding loosely to convictions comes from the concept of a golf swing. When one grips a golf club in preparation for a swing, it is important not to grip the club too tightly. If you do, you tense the rest of the muscles in your arm, which in turn, messes up the rest of the swing. It doesn't mean that your hands are loose around the club; after all, you need to enough of a grip so that the when you do swing, it's the ball, and not the club, that flies. So, you firmly, but loosely, hold the club so that the process of holding the club doesn't interfere with the rest of the swing motion.

So how does this concept apply to holding onto your convictions? It doesn't mean that you allow yourself to be easily persuaded against what you believe. It means that you are so convinced of what you believe that the other person's words cannot goad you into an argument. It means that you can really listen to what their heart is saying and not just look for points to argue. It means you are free to see the person behind the opinion.

leaves

To hold loosely to your beliefs, keep in mind that God deliberately leaving Himself open to disbelief. "It is the glory of God to conceal a matter and it is the glory of a king to search out a matter."[5] Think about it for a minute. God, if He wanted, could remove all cause for doubt. Instead, He conceals things so that we will search them out. He could make it so obvious it would be impossible not to believe. He could have created in us a nature that would not doubt, but He didn't.

When you can understand this, you can understand that not believing is a choice God has allowed. Or, put another way, if God gives people room to doubt Him, how can you or I do any less? By trusting what you believe, and at the same time allowing them the freedom of

---

[5] Prov. 25.2 NET

others

their doubts about what you believe, you begin to hold your convictions loosely. You believe what you believe deeply, but you are free to allow the other person their doubts, express their worldviews and explore their reasons for disbelief.

Just as you and I hold to our conviction in God's Word, people who are not Christ followers have (what they believe) strong reasons for keeping God at a distance, rejecting God (though they may believe He exists) or even rejecting that He exists. Why? Can't they see how a relationship with God can bring personal peace, world peace? Can't they see in the world around them how intricate nature is, how intricate our bodies are? How can they see that and not conclude there is a Master Creator? For every reason you have for believing in God, your friend, your conversation partner has a reason for thinking you are...nuts.

They hold to their beliefs as strongly as you hold to yours. For you, Christ is the core. For them, something or someone else is worth staking their lives on. What explains this difference in

[handwritten margin notes: "use short sentences rather than parentheses" "or delete them?" "these things"]

comma rather than dash?

Maybe leave out question of either?

convictions? The answer to this is what we began this chapter with - our experiences, our hopes and our disappointments. These shape how we look at the world around us and how we interpret the information we see.

Redundant

Keep this in mind – this information we all see is neutral. It is neither good nor is it bad. You and I, based on how we interpret the information we see, assign the good or bad label. Let me share an example. Today, the possibility of someone strapping explosives to their body, walking into a crowd and killing themselves, and those around them, has become an unpleasant fact. Now, before I go forward, take a minute and think about your reactions. I'll wait.

What were your reactions?

Did you feel sadness? Did anger cross your heart? Maybe you are one who has lost a loved one to one of these acts. I am sorry for the pain of that loss. But, believe it or not, there are individuals for whose emotions are at the opposite end of the emotional spectrum. They might feel admiration, excitement or even praise for the bomber's actions. To you and me, this extreme difference of how we view that act, that bomber can be incomprehensible. The act is neutral – it is you and I how assign the "good" or "bad" label.

we

But, as incomprehensible as it may be, we need to understand that others hold to their beliefs as deeply as we do and the convictions of their belief may be stronger than ours. If we cannot grasp this concept, then sharing our faith will be a frustrating experience. If we can grasp this concept, I believe it will also allow us to hold our convictions loosely and allow us to hear what they are saying. *We will connect with*

Our clearest body of evidence about God comes from the Bible. We have to understand that though the words on the pages of a Bible are the same, there is a great deal of difference in how we interpret them. I happened to come across a documentary of Jonathon Sharkey. He ran for president in 2004 and 2008 ~~as well for a~~ variety of other political offices. He is also a self-proclaimed vampire and Satanist. He believes in God, but he rejects Him. He believes he cannot

them as the golf club will connect with the ball. (?)

and a

worship a God who allowed children to die and who cruelly killed His own Son, even turning His back on Jesus as He hung on the cross. Now, these words are found in the Gospels. They are plainly laid out. Neither Jonathon nor I will disagree that Jesus did die a horrible death on the cross. We can agree that on the cross, Jesus cried out in despair as He, for the first time, felt the separation from His Father. Jonathon and I (and you) are reading the same words.

But the difference is the meaning, the value we attach to those words. Jonathon sees this as a description of evil and rejects God's love. I see Christ's execution as the most beautiful thing that has ever been done for me. God didn't kill His son. He did allow Him to die, but Jesus' death was His own choice. God honored that choice in a) allowing it to happen and b) bringing Jesus back from the death three days later. I believe the event happened; so does Jonathon. Our difference is in how we understand the meaning of the event.

This same principle applies to all evidence, all information. What you see as proof there is

God, another sees the same information and believes it disproves God. We see this in the debate between Creation and evolution. We see it in the exchanges between archeology and theology. We even see it in the diversity of different denominations. We see it in faiths that say they believe the Bible, but add or significantly distort their understanding of what it says. The Bible is the Bible. It has been translated, revised, updated to modern language, but the message has not changed in over 2,000 years.

Where does that leave you and me when it comes to sharing our faith? First, as we said earlier, you have to know why you believe in Christ. What is it that convinces you that with all the other possibilities out there, Jesus is only the Truth that set you (and anyone else) free, *eleuthroo*?

Second, accept that no matter how strong your convictions, how solid you feel about your reasoning, they are not enough to change someone else's core belief. Your life, your conviction, your words may raise questions,

doubts in the other person, but you alone are
not enough to address that person's
experiences, hopes and disappointments. A
non-Believer will have their reasons for their
beliefs. They will probably not call it a belief —
they could call it logic, they could call it
scientific, it could be emotional. They will have
their own label for their belief. "Secret things
belong to the LORD our God, but those that are
revealed belong to us and our descendants
forever, so that we might obey all the words of
this law.[6]" Given that God has kept some things
hidden from us, we have to accept that we will
not have enough facts to prove our point. That's
OK.

Jesus spent three years pouring into His
disciples' lives and they still didn't get it.
Recently, the words of Mark 9:10 struck me. As
Jesus is leaving His transfiguration experience,
He instructs Peter, James and John not to tell
anyone what they saw until "after the Son of
Man had risen from the dead (v.9) V.10 says,
"So they kept it to themselves, but they often

---

[6] Deut. 29.29

asked themselves what He meant by 'raising from the dead'". If Jesus' words and miracles could not penetrate their experiences, their hopes and their disappointments until after they experienced His resurrection, can we expect to do any better?

Third, instead of looking at the surface arguments, ask God to let you hear the person's heart. Something in their experiences, their hopes, their disappointments has given a home to their arguments against belief in God.

Finally, remember, it's not about winning an argument, of proving the other person wrong. It's about being a vessel for God's love, His Spirit ministering to the other person's experiences, hopes and disappointments. It's about God wanting to enter into relationship with that person.

When your goal is to win the discussion, the focus is on you, not God. When that happens, you both loose.

When you goal is to share Christ, the focus is Christ. *Eleuthroo* is near.

Knowing God

For every tragedy, difficulty, pain or confusion in life, there is the question of, "LORD, what are You doing?" Some Believers will say these questions are signs of sin or lack of faith. Others might point to them as trials that strengthen a believer's character. The challenging fact is that most times, Scripture has no definitive answer to this question. God works in our lives as He best sees fit. "Then the LORD answered Job: Will the one who contends with the Almighty correct Him? Let the person who accuses God give Him an answer."[7] God has no need or requirement to explain Himself. However, there is another element to the soul shaking issues in our lives I'd like to suggest—these struggles are a gift from God.

I wouldn't be honest if I didn't say that I struggle to appreciate the gift. As someone who has always preferred the easy way out, I can

---

[7] Job 40 1-2

Amen

honestly say I would prefer a less stressful, soul-sapping gift. But, intellectually, I also, know that God does not give any "bad" gifts. So, what is the gift? A stronger character? A deeper faith? A deeper intimacy with God? I would say yes, but it's more than any or even all of these.

In John 14, Jesus is comforting His disciples as He prepares for His crucifixion the next day. He tells them He is going to prepare a place for them. He says, "If you really knew Me, you would know My Father, as well.[8]" Philip asks Jesus to show them the Father and that will be good enough for them. Jesus' response is cutting and shows the heart of His desire for us.

He responds, "Don't you know me, Philip, even after I have been among you for such a long time? Anyone who has seen Me has seen the Father"[9]. This passage, tucked into a wealth of memory verses, reveals the heart of God's desire – that we really know Him.

---

[8] John 14.7
[9] John 14.9

This knowing is not simply a study of the Bible combined with reading good authors and attending insightful studies. We can spend lots of time gaining an in depth education on God, Jesus, the Holy Spirit, the Second Coming and a variety of other important theological topics. But all the information available will not fulfill Jesus' desire that we know Him. It can help us know about Him, but knowing Him is something more, a completely different level that cannot be reached by intellect alone. What do I mean?

In college, I took a Philosophy of Religions class. The professor was so brilliant I still have very little idea of what he was teaching. However, there is one concept I did walk away with. It is the concept of Shared Experience. Basically, in order for you to understand what I am trying to describe, you need to have shared the experience with me. If not, there are aspects of the experience I will not be able to convey – smells, feelings, emotions. You may understand if you have had a similar experience, but it still will be missing some elements of what I'm trying to share if it's not the same experience.

I grew up as a missionary kid with my parents moving often. A major portion of their work was in refugee care. Even now, trying to share with people what growing up on the move or working in a refugee camp is frustrating because I can't convey everything. My wife & I nearly lost our son, twice, in auto accidents before he was five. We also know parents who have lost their children to disease, accidents or suicide. Even though we went through the experience of nearly losing a child, I cannot honestly say I understand the depth of pain our friends have experienced. And, no matter how many books I might read on loss and grief, I will come no closer to that understanding.

This is what Jesus is trying to convey to His disciples here. After all their time together, they still do really know Him. They know of His power, they have heard Him teach and have even seen His heart as He cried over a dead friend, a doomed city. Yet, they still do not know their rabbi, their teacher. Their own ideas, their own wants, their own misconceptions kept getting in the way of a true relationship with Jesus.

And it is not as if there is any deep, double meaning to the word used for "to know". The original Greek is *"ginosko"* (Strong's 1097). It means to learn to know, to understand, to perceive, to feel...to know. Jesus is asking His disciples how, after all the experiences they have shared together over the last three years, they still do know understand what He is about, the still do not perceive His mission here on Earth. How can Philip have spent so much time in His presence and still not grasp the divine nature of Jesus?

And today, that same cry of Jesus still echoes for you and I...If you really knew me. How do we begin to truly know Jesus, to know the Father? By sharing Their experiences. By feeling a small portion of what They feel. And that is not something I can honestly say I always welcome. Sure, I want to share God's joy when someone invites Jesus to be Lord or when a prodigal returns. There is a great celebration and count me in. But...what about God's pain at watching His Son being abandoned, beaten and crucified. Do I really want to feel the disappointment of Jesus as He watched His friends run away into the night as He was being dragged off to the illegal trial? Do I really look forward to being in a situation where I look to Heaven and cry out, "My God, my God, why have you forsaken me?" Do I really want to be in a place where I feel the depth of pain God experiences as He watches His children daily reject Him? What about the pain of Jesus as we mock the sacrifice He made so we could be able to know God through our sinful behaviors?

I am not saying you or I will ever experience the magnitude of what God feels. We can't. But we can feel what He feels on a scale that is significant for us. As I languish in a long period of time where it seems like my prayers go unanswered, I can begin to relate it to the cry of the Son who felt abandoned on the cross. When friends seem to ignore the challenges I face, I can have a glimpse at what Jesus might have felt as He stood alone in the Garden of Gethsemane, facing the troop of soldiers ready to take Him away.

During these challenging times, it is easy to feel God is punishing me or has left me on my own. It is easy to be frustrated because the faith I have doesn't seem be enough to turn the situation around. Christians you know scratch their heads and try to figure out why prayers seem to remain unanswered. And it is in these times it can be tempting to feel faith in God is pointless.

On the other hand, I can respond by realizing God is giving me the gift of knowing Him; not knowing about Him, but giving me a glimpse of His thoughts, His feelings, of who He is. He is giving me the gift of a shared experience.

And, in all honesty, I can't always say I appreciate that gift. I can't honestly say I always appreciate the struggles, the pain, the worry that comes in these times. I know...we're told not to worry, to rejoice in affliction and pain. But keep in mind, if not worrying, if being joyful in affliction and pain was easy, God would not spend time in His Word laying out how we should respond to these challenges in our lives.

In closing out this thought, ask yourself this, "When my circumstances seem to be pulling me down, when my prayers seem to be unanswered, when I look around and see only me, do I see the gift wrapped in the pain?" This does not mean the circumstances will immediately change. Unemployment may continue, a sick child may not be healed, a relationship may continue to be strained or whatever else is being experienced may continue to weigh on your heart. But, in the continued experience, we can look at it as God saying, "I trust you to share My heart with you so that you may know me better than any book ever will."

What's My Nehushtan?

I was reading the story of Hezekiah's cleaning up of Judah's religious practices in 2 Kings 18 not too long ago and was struck by one of his actions. Verse 4 describes him leading the destruction of the high places, sacred stones and Asherah poles. These were all items that were used to worship the idols which the Hebrews had adopted from their neighbors over the centuries. This was not the first time a revival had taken place, but there was something that Hezekiah had added to the destruction pile, something that had not come from their neighbors. It was the Nehushtan, the bronze serpent God had commanded Moses to make.

A quick flash back – in Numbers 21.4-9, the Israelites are once again complaining about the journey they are taking from Egypt to Canaan. They complain against God and against Moses. They are angry, sarcastic and impatient. And

God is not pleased. He sends poisonous snakes into their camp on a biting rampage. As people begin to die, the general population realizes they have sinned and repent. They beg Moses to intercede with God on their behalf. God's response is to have Moses make a bronze snake, lift it up on a pole and set it where anyone who had been bitten can look up, see it and be healed.

We don't hear any more of the snake until this 2 King's passage. The Israelites had kept it all those centuries. It could have been a reminder to be thankful, to not grumble, a reminder of God's healing or something else. Scripture doesn't say exactly why they kept it. What this passage does indicate is that somewhere between the wanderings in the desert and the reign of Hezekiah, the bronze snake, called the Nehushtan, had evolved from a symbol of God's redemption into an object of misplaced worship. Again, we don't know the nature of that worship; only that it had become an idol, something that was receiving the type of attention that belongs only to God.

It got me to thinking about whom and what I worship today. What takes my attention that rightfully only belongs to God? Yes, we probably do not have a sacred stone or an altar or a pole in our homes. That doesn't mean we don't have something with which God has blessed us that we have begun to place as more important than Him. No, you think? Let me throw out a couple of examples.

Family is something high on God's list of good things. Yet, family life can become something that can receive the attention that belongs to God alone. How is that possible? Well, have you ever found that you were prioritizing family events over opportunities to be involved in serving in your church? I am not saying that all church service is more important than being with family. But is there a balance? Do you involve your family in church service? Or, are you teaching your kids they can be used to justify not becoming more involved in what your church is doing to reach out to its community?

How about finances? It is common, though inaccurate, to think that because we are financially secure, God is blessing us. It's inaccurate because there are grossly immoral individuals who are financially secure. At the same time, there are Godly people who struggle on a daily basis. Paul talked about times when he was in need as well as when he had plenty. And, he ended his life in prison, being executed for his faith. In terms of today's definition of God's blessings, this doesn't seem to fit.

So, how about your finances? What does your checkbook look like? If God challenged you to take on support of a missionary, would you do so willingly? If someone in your church was struggling with finding work, would you be willing to help them make ends meet? If God asked you to simplify your life to free up more of your resources for Him, what would be your response?

We can go on. In marriage, is your spouse more important than God? Are you a source of division in your church because of the music or the building fund or because you don't like one of the pastors? What about a ministry? Is proving Creation more important than building a relationship with an evolutionist that honors God? The list can go on. All have something good, something God placed there for your good. But, somewhere along the way, that person or thing or situation became more important that God.

Most of us probably don't realize we've let that happen. I doubt any of us consciously decided that our family was more important than serving God. Same with the finances, the music, the you name it. But, let someone bring it up now, and you're ready to get into an argument, to defend your choices. You may already be ready to disagree with me in the examples I've put here.

It is important to realize that the bronze snake itself was never the problem. Its original purpose was for restitution. It was used by God to bring healing. Jesus, in John 3.14-15, would use it as an analogy for what His death would do for us. So, the original purpose of the Nehushtan was not in question. What was in question was the value that people put on it. And that is the same for us today. Families are not bad, marriage is not bad, money is not bad. The same is true for ministries, styles of worship, church decorations or any number of other issues in our lives. The issue, the transformation from good to bad, comes from within us, within our hearts.

It is us, you and I, who place our family on the altar ahead of God. It is me who is more concerned about my spouse than my Father. We thank God for a positive bank account, but then refuse to release it to Him for His use when He asks. We might not sing hymns to our family, we might not pray to our spouse, we might not try to share how our finances saved us. But, how we respond when God asks us which is more important will let us know what is most important in our hearts.

So, what do we do? First, we need to ask God if we have a Nehushtan in our lives. Be careful. You need to be prepared to find a response that will be difficult. You may find that His answer will seem to contradict what has been taught by someone you trust. Or, you may find you took a good teaching too far. Regardless, if you want God to answer this prayer, be ready for an answer you might not like.

Then, you need to ask Him how to best move forward. It may not involve physical smashing, but something is going to get broken. You may need to confess to your spouse what has happened. You may need to change your family's schedule. You might have to downsize – a house, a car, some toys, I don't know. You may need to have coffee with a pastor or a Bible study leader to see where you may have missed something in what they taught. I don't know...but God does. Trust Him in the process. Focus on placing His gifts in the proper perspective.

Hezekiah's heart was focused on doing what was right in the LORD's eyes (v3). He trusted in the LORD (v5). He eliminated the idols his people had raised in place of God. And God honored that. The question for you and I today is where is our focus? Is it on God or His gifts? Those questions can only be answered when you seek His answer.

Sacrifice or Worldly Things

"He...had no quarrel with his religion, and its rituals and ceremonies provided him the comfort of a childhood blanket. But he ignored any teaching that got in the way of his enjoyment of worldly things. He also worked most Sabbaths because his job required it."[10]

I came across this paragraph in a novel. The part about ignoring any teaching that got in the way of his enjoyment of worldly things seemed to sum up how many of us put our faith into action. I am not talking about the obvious situations of people who profess Christ, but put out no effort beyond looking the part of a Christian.

I am talking about the individual who is serious in wanting to deepen their relationship with God, but find it difficult to scale back, or cut out, their way of life in order to be used by God

---

[10] Silva, Daniel, The Marching Season pg. 87

more. They maintain a lifestyle that is more than comfortable. If you ask them how their life is, they say they are blessed, enjoying life and couldn't be happier. They have their vacations, their kids in all types of clubs and are busy planning the next event in their church, their community or their family. But in all of that, one word that does not come up is "sacrifice"...unless it is part of a joke, "Well somebody has got to go on that nice trip. I'll do it but it's a sacrifice".

I admit that word "sacrifice" doesn't bring up warm fuzzy feelings in me. In the Western world, I don't see that the full weight of that word even seeps into our conscious. God calls us to be living sacrifices - "Therefore I exhort you, brothers and sisters, by the mercies of God, to present your bodies as a sacrifice – alive, holy and pleasing to God – which is your reasonable service."[11] Yet, if we don't fully

---

[11] Rom. 12.1 New English Translation

understand the weight of that word, how can we fulfill this call?

The word "sacrifice" comes from the Greek *thuos* (Strong's – 2378) and means victim. It is rooted in the word *thuo* (Strong's – 2380) which is defined as immolate, slay, kill, slaughter. It loses the weight of its meaning in a Western culture where sacrifice is not a regular way of life. In the culture of the Old & New Testament, it meant a life was lost for the benefit of another. In Biblical times, most religious practices, including Judaism, used animals to take the place of humans. In order for communication between man and their deity to take place, blood had to be shed. A victim had to be killed, slaughtered, immolated (burned) or otherwise deprived of its life.

This dynamic is true for us as Christians – "For the payoff of sin is death, but the gift of God is eternal life in Christ Jesus our Lord"[12]. We have

---

[12] Rom. 6.23 NET

all sinned; the payoff is death. We must have a sacrifice to pay the penalty if we do not want to pay the penalty ourselves. Because of God's love and mercy, there is a perfect sacrifice.

This good news, or Gospel, is that Jesus agreed to be that sacrifice. He chose to be the sacrifice to be slaughtered so that His blood would permit the direct communication between God & us. But, because few of us have ever seen a sacrifice, it is difficult to fully understand the depth of meaning in this word word and how it applies to us.

I was visiting Kolkata, India several years ago. I visited the house of the dying set up by Mother Teresa. She had deliberately set it up next to the main temple of Kali, the Hindu deity of destruction. After a tour of the house, I went next door to the temple where I watched as family after family came forward with a goat, a sheep or some other animal and handed their sacrifice over to the priests. The animal was locked into a stock, a sword flashed and the head was cut off. A bowl was used to collect the blood which was then dabbed on the foreheads of the family members. A victim had been slaughtered so the communication between the family and Kali could be completed.

What does this have to do with us? It is a description, which even as I write it several years later, still stirs conflicting emotions in me. But in looking at our discussion, the question I ask is this – what do I sacrifice for my King? Am I really grateful that I no longer have to take an animal to a temple so that God will hear me, forgive me? Do I fully understand that because of Jesus' sacrifice on the Cross, I do not have to pay the penalty for my sin. But, in not having to do that, have I lost the weight of what it means to sacrifice? Has it become easy for me to ignore any of Christ's teachings that get in the way of me enjoying worldly things?

These are not easy questions to answer. But, this cannot prevent me from offering up a loving challenge to both you and me...are there teachings you and I ignore because they get in the way of worldly things? Who do I bounce that question off of so that I don't lie to myself? When was the last time I looked around to see if I really needed the size of house, or class of car, or number of trips, or clothes...or whatever it might be that I enjoy more than God? What in my life would be a sacrifice to surrender so that I might grow in my relation with Christ?

It is important to remember here that God wants you and me to come forward and ask Him this question. And, it is also important to keep in mind that when we do ask, it will hurt. That is the nature of a sacrifice. I have talked about material things, but maybe it is pride He wants sacrificed. Ouch! Maybe it is a child to ministry somewhere far from you. Oh LORD, not that. Maybe He wants you to give up a heart of hurt, of bitterness towards someone else. But LORD, don't You remember what that person did? I have a right these feelings.

I don't know what He is calling you to sacrifice. It could be something material, it could be emotional, it could be something else. But, the question you and I have to ask is this, "What is more important – that worldly thing(s) or His Word, His Teaching, Him.

"LORD, teach me again the meaning of sacrifice that I may more fully understand the meaning of the Cross. As I learn the true depth of that word, then please reveal worldly things I should sacrifice for Your sake. Amen."

The Balance of Faith

One of the most challenging dynamics about faith and the Christian life is it is a balancing act. When fully lived out, a faith in Christ can seem to be, at times, contradictory. Jesus tells us to keep on asking and we shall receive (Matt. 7:7). This is just after He tells us not to worry about what we'll eat or drink or wear because of our Father's loving care for us (Matt. 6:31). So, which is it – keep asking or stop worrying (I wouldn't ask if I wasn't worrying)?

The answers that come from human sources can range everywhere from "God is strengthening your faith" to "if you just really believed God's promises, you wouldn't be_____ (sick, poor, alone, kids struggling...you fill in the blank)". Finding an explanation, a label seems to give us something we can blame or something we can do to change our situation.

But a lack of faith, or an immature faith, doesn't always correspond Biblically. If it did, then why would Paul say that he had learned to live with almost nothing or with everything,...on an empty stomach or full, with plenty or little (Phil. 4:12)? When he was hungry, or had almost nothing, was it because he didn't have faith in God?

Others will claim that sin in our lives is what keeps us in whatever condition it was that you filled in the blank earlier. While I can agree that sometimes God does allow the consequences of my actions to get my attention, it again doesn't make sense in light of scripture. We ALL have sin in our life. 1 John 1:8, "If we claim we have no sin, we are only fooling ourselves and not living in the truth." Yes, if we confess our sins, God is faithful and just and forgives our sins, but it won't take long before we sin again. It's not that we're looking to, it's just because we are human. Just look at Paul's frustration in Rom. 7. "I don't really understand myself. I want to do what is right, but I can't. Instead, I do what I hate" (v.14).

And it goes on. Just when I seem to have a solid answer to why my life is in so much turmoil, the Bible points out several other options. It's no wonder so many throw up their hands and either never fully explore what Christ offers or try for a bit only to find it too hard and walk away. The reality is your situation is different from mine. What God wants to develop in your relationship with Him is unique to you. Your Bible study partner may have been miraculously delivered from nicotine addiction while you struggle on an hourly basis not to light up. I can ask God why He spared my son's life in an auto accident years ago while the driver, a dear friend, died of his injuries. Whose faith was stronger? Was mine stronger than my friend's family and friends? Did God love my wife and me more than them?

The answer to those questions is no. God loves each of us with everything He has. He sent His

Son Jesus, to pay the death sentence we all carry. He didn't set aside a certain percentage of the World's population and say to the rest of us, "Sorry, I can't love anymore". 1 Peter 3:18 – Christ died once for all our sins. John 3:16 – "For God so loved the <u>world</u> that He gave His only Son that <u>everyone</u> who believes in Him will not perish but have eternal life (underline mine)."

"God has His favorites", some will say. David was called the Friend of God. Moses was buried by God in a secret place. Enoch and Elijah didn't die; God took them up before their death. Mary was called Favored One by the angel. It is true that these individuals devoted themselves to seeking God. David followed God with all His heart. Moses was credited with being the humblest man. Enoch walked closely with God and Elijah repeatedly put His life on the line to call the Israelites to repentance. Mary was chosen to be the mother of Jesus.

But, you can rebut, for every Elijah, how many other prophets were tortured and killed for doing the same work? What made David's desire for God stronger than his friend Jonathan's? Enoch walked in close fellowship with God, but so have many others over the last several millennium. What makes him so special? And of the eleven disciples Jesus selected, all but one were martyred killed for their faith. The answer is there is no one answer, at least none that God "has" to give us. He does not owe us anything, let alone need to explain himself. And this is where faith comes into testing.

Deuteronomy 29:29 says, "The LORD our God has secrets known to no one. We are not accountable for them, but we and our children are accountable forever for all that He has revealed to us, so that we may obey all the terms of His instructions." Quite simply, we will not know all the answers to our questions. We can have answers for why we think things are happening in our lives, or in others lives, but we have to treat those thoughts carefully. We have to have awareness we could very well be wrong.

You only have to read the book of Job to see that.

Job was a righteous man, blessed of God. He has family, health and wealth. God boasts of Job's faithfulness to Satan. Satan challenges God that Job's love is conditional; he loves God because of what God has given Job. Take it all away, Satan claims, and Job would sing a different song. God gives Satan permission to take it all away – wealth, kids, reputation; everything but his life. When Satan strikes, his friends come, convinced that something in Job's life is to the reason for his sudden downfall. Surely there is some sin, something Job has done that has displeased God. But Job knows there isn't. He holds fast to God in spite of his circumstances, his friends' challenges and his wife's ridicule. He proclaims his innocence.

Finally, God enters the conversation in the last couple of chapters to challenge Job, to challenge the human attempts to find an answer God has kept secret. The summary of

God's challenge to Job is, "Who do you think you are? I don't need anyone to 'defend' Me to anyone. If you can do what I do, then you can challenge Me." Next thing we know, God has restored Job's blessings.

For me, it's important to note that God did not ever say that any of the friends were wrong in their advice (because we know we all sin) nor did He condemn Job's wife for criticizing her husband. At the same time, He never confirmed their feelings. He also never revealed why it was Job went through what he went through. What He did do was define our relationship with Him. If you can do everything God can, then you may have a right to expect an explanation. Until then, He is God; we are not.

That, to me, is the heart of my struggle of faith. It's when I look at God's promise to provide, then at the bills stacked next to the rejected employment applications and choose not to lose hope. Faith gives us assurance of what we cannot see. I can look at what I perceive as a "lack" of God's provision right now or I can choose to focus on His Word where Jesus promises me that God will take care of my needs as I put His Kingdom first. It seems easy to trust when I have more money in my account than what the bills say I need. I pay them and I go on my merry way. It's when I see the negative that I have to choose to have faith in my Father and His word.

Some teach that God does not want us to suffer. If we are sick, just speak the name of Jesus and believe you are healed. If we lack something we need, claim it in the name of Jesus and it is ours. Jesus gave us all authority in Heaven and on Earth. He said we would do even greater things than He did. The book of Acts records where people came to the apostles because of their ability to heal. I have personally experienced God's miracles in healing, in provision, in protection. I have also known and know times of want, of need, of sickness. Does that mean I have lost my faith, lost my strength to believe? As I write, I struggle with this thought. This is a season of need. It is a season of testing. It is the type of season God allows to strengthen my endurance, to build my faith stronger; it is the type of season where I struggle to be content as Paul challenges me to be. Can I be thankful? I can if I am willing to step back from myself and thank God for what He is allowing. James 1:12 reminds me, "God blesses those who patiently endure testing and temptation. Afterward they will receive the crown of life that God has promised those who love Him."

Endurance, testing, temptation. Not words I can honestly say I thrill to have associated with my life's circumstances. I prefer the quiet streams, the cool pastures, the unstressful seasons of life. It is so much easier to have faith when faith is not needed. I am so much more confident in God's promises when I don't have to rely solely on those promises. As Peter found out, it so much easier to have faith in Jesus when you are in the boat than when you are walking down a windy valley of waves towering over you.

For me, Peter in the boat then walking on the water sums up the debate within the body of Christ. Does God always provide the boat? If we are in the stormy sea, with nothing to hold us from sinking, do we claim the boat is there or believe that if we speak to the wind and the waves, they will calm down? Even as I write this, I just received an e-mail from a former colleague from when my wife and I worked in Guinea. Just yesterday, she asked for prayer that her son, now in college, would find a job. My wife & I have been sharing a similar request, but for our kids and for me. Today, her son has work. It took 6 months of praying for my son to find a job, my daughter is still looking and I've been looking for full time work for nearly 5 years.

Does that mean I don't believe in God's promises? Does that mean my faith is less than our colleagues? It doesn't take much; just a mustard seed full to move mountains from here to there (Matt. 17:20). Does God love our colleagues more than us? Nothing in His word gives that indication. How do I react to this "discrepancy"? I can get angry, frustrated, anxious, envious, pout, you name it. Or, I can see this as an opportunity to strengthen my faith. God commands you and I to rejoice with those who rejoice. It does not say, "...if we're in a good mood." Nor does it say "...well, if you're still waiting for a similar response, you can sit this one out." No, it says "Be happy with those who are happy,...(Romans 12:15).

So I am going to be happy for my friends. I am going to praise God He provided work for their son. The minute I start to feel sorry for myself or my daughter, I'm going to again quote God's command – Be happy with those who are happy.

And this, I believe, is the heart of the faith balance. Faith isn't something that just happens. It isn't something that you quote a verse or make a decleration and poof, your troubles are gone. No, it is a day-by-day choice to look at God, to obey His commands, to believe His promises when everything in you screams to run the other way. Does that mean I always succeed? I wish! Oh that I could easily sing Hosanna when God's blessings on my brother next to me are so evident. I wish that when I looked at the waves that seem to be about to engulf me I could calmly watch them instead of sink underneath them in fear.

But I'm not perfect. I do sink. Then what? Well, Prov. 26:14 says, "The Godly will trip seven times, but they will get up again." I will trip; so will you. The question is do I want to remain on the ground or do I want to get up so God can provide another chance to strengthen my faith? Do I want my faith strengthened? That is the question we have to face, to answer honestly. Remember the guys we talked about earlier...David, Moses, Elijah? They weren't always perfect in their faith. They had family problems. People wanted their heads. They sinned spectacularly. In moments of weakness, they ran. As some would say today, they lacked faith in crucial moments of their lives. But, they got back up. They went back at it.

And, as for the question of how quickly God keeps His promises, the answer isn't always what I'd like. Sometimes it was immediately; other times, He took His time. How long did David wait from the time he was anointed before God granted him Israel's throne? There were times he could have "speeded up" the process, but he didn't. God promised him the kingdom. David believed God would keep His promise. But that belief wasn't rewarded instantaneously. It took years to happen. And God is the same today. Some promises are fulfilled before the cry is out of our heart. Others wear holes in our knees as we wait in eager expectation for His fulfillment. If there is any answer to this dilemma, I feel it is found in the nature of God's reply to Job and his "friends".

I believe it is simply this: God is God and we are not. God is not ours to order around, to guilt into meeting our needs. He doesn't respond to an incantation. No magic phrase will bring us the answer we desire. This is because God is not ours to order around. In our human nature, it would be too easy to slide into the mode of seeing God as a genie. We rub His lamp and get our three wishes. I'd like to think that I wouldn't fall into that, but remember, if I had my choice, I'd prefer the calm sunset on the lake to the violent storm crashing over the bow.

So, how do I reconcile the Scriptures that teach that all I have to do is claim my authority over whatever I am facing and it will be taken care of with times like now where I cry out and I call out and nothing seems to happen? I have learned to step back from the specific passages and look, instead, at His whole Word. When I do that, I see both. I see the miracles, the healings, the instant provision. I also see the friend of God who waited years to take his place as king. I see Daniel praying for his people to be released but that not happening in his lifetime. I see God promising Abraham to be a great nation, but not in His lifetime. And in looking at the whole picture, I can see the fulcrum of the balance is God's will.

And that is the key...His will. Ask Jesus as He knelt on a cold, lonely night, praying that God would have another, hidden plan, one that Jesus didn't know about. Praying that once again, like Abraham and Isaac so long ago, God was waiting till the last moment to pull out something else. When He didn't, Jesus had a choice. He could have gotten up and walked out of the garden and disappeared into the mists of history. Most likely we would never have heard of him. His followers would have woken up when the temple guards arrived and would honestly have had no clue as to where He had gone.

His other choice was the exercise of His faith, His trust in His Father. "Your will be done." No claiming of His authority over the circumstances He was facing . No rebuking of the forces of Satan arrayed against Him. He knew He could. Matt. 26:53, "Don't you realize I could ask my Father for thousands of angels to protect us, and He would send them instantly?" Instead, He trusted that God knew all things. If angels were needed to fulfill God's plan, angels would have been there. But, instead, there was just Jesus and the soldiers sent to capture Him. Jesus trusted Himself to the will of His Father. The rest is history; not one lost in the mists of time but blazed across the world for all to see.

So, as I look at the challenges in my life, I want to approach them with boldness. I choose to claim God's victory now. I choose to believe He is not slow to keep His promise and trust that His timing is perfect. Sometimes, there will be answers, healings, and rescues immediately. There will also be times where I call and call and nothing seems to happen. It is in these times God is giving me the chance, and the choice, to allow my faith to grow.

The Ends of the Earth

A key part of having a faith, a belief, is sharing it with others. As a Christ follower, sharing is part of what you and I are supposed to do. After all, we have read the Last Chapter so we know how our story ends. We believed it to the extent of confessing our sins, accepting that Jesus paid our sins' penalty and committing to a life that is focused on God, His love for us and how He planned for each of us to live. A part of that plan is following Jesus' instructions on sharing God's love. His last instruction - "But you will receive power when the Holy Spirit comes upon you. And you will be My witnesses, telling people about Me everywhere – in Jerusalem, throughout Judea, in Samaria, and to the ends of the earth."[13]

This passage is used frequently when the sermon subject is missions or community

---

[13] Acts 1:8 New Living Translation

outreaches. The common application of this passage is geographical - Jerusalem being your neighborhood or town, Judea being your county or your region, Samaria your country and the ends of the earth, well the rest of the world. But recently, in looking at this passage, a different angle, a personal, day-to-day application of this passage came into focus.

The first thing that is new for me is the word "witness". I am to be His witness. When I hear that word, the first image that comes to mind is opening a conversation with, "Have you heard the Good News?" I also think of someone sitting in the witness box at a trial, telling the jury what they saw. But then I looked the word up in Strong's. The original Greek word is *martus* (Strong's Greek - 3144). *Martrus* is more than starting a conversation about God. It is more than swearing to tell the truth, the whole truth and nothing but the truth.

When you look up *martrus* in Strong's, there are several definitions. They include the definitions listed above, but there is another definition of the word challenges me – "those who after His example have proved the strength and genuineness of their faith by undergoing a violent death". Say what?!? I have to think about that for a minute. The Greek word for witness is also the word that gives us "martyr". Jesus is saying that He wants me to be ready to prove my faith by being ready for a violent death. Great! Where do I sign up?

In this last instruction, Jesus uses three distinct geographical places and one general. For the Jewish person, each of these places is symbolic as well as physical. And, like "witness", there are additional meanings to the symbolic phrase "ends of the earth". Let's take them in order.

Jerusalem was as close to Heaven on earth as one could get in the Jewish faith. Even today, when the Passover is celebrated anywhere but in Jerusalem, the phrase, "Next year in Jerusalem" is included. In Jesus' time, Jerusalem was the place to be. The temple was there. Government was there. If you had the choice of living anywhere, it would be...Jerusalem. So, in this perspective, "Jerusalem" can be seen as my comfort zone.

This is where I am comfortable being a Jesus witness. It could be family and friends who know me and like me anyway. It could be a situation where I know that what I say won't be judged. I'll be listened to, but even if those who are listening don't agree, we can agree to disagree and still enjoy each other's company. I can live out what I believe and feel safe. This is my Jerusalem.

From there, I move out to Judea. Here, in this new approach in looking at Jesus' challenge, my comfort zone is being stretched. I'm being pushed to the edge of my comfort zone; there will probably be times I will go outside of it. In this area, the boundaries of my comfort zone could be extended by the time all is said and done.

What might this look like? Have you ever been asked to share your testimony with a large group of people? What about telling an authority figure you admire about your belief in Jesus, especially if they aren't a believer? How about when you first placed your faith in Jesus? What was that like when you shared it with friends and family? These situations are all areas where you are sharing your faith in a familiar arena, but you aren't sure what the reaction will be.

Pushing boundaries can be scary. I am risking maybe some stares, someone thinking I'm a bit out there, maybe even risking a friendship. A part of me could figuratively die...of embarrassment. I am moving into areas where I probably won't feel completely safe in living what I believe. Jesus calls us to die to ourselves. This is where I begin to die to myself, even if it is just a little bit.

Samaria is the next arena in Jesus's expanding challenge. How can Samaria be seen in this light? Samaria was the last place any respectable Jew would want to go. The Jews looked down on the Samaritans, despised them. Some historians have pointed out a really devout Jew preferred to walk a couple of extra days on their journey to go around Samaria to avoid any association with the place and its people.

If I am honest with myself, I have to admit there are Samarias in my life. There are probably a few in yours, too. If you don't agree, let me ask you this. Are you good friends with someone who is homosexual? Do you count drug addicts among those you have to dinner? What about places you avoid going? Do you believe no Christian should ever go into a bar? Does that person who is visiting your church fit in with the subconscious profile of a desirable new member?

Let me add a clarification here. There are some places individual Christians should avoid if any of those places, and to a lesser extent, people, pose a serious threat. What do I mean? One example would be a Christian who is also a recovering alcoholic. Going into a bar may not be a good idea. A recovering drug addict may need to avoid active users. But, before anyone makes a blanket statement, keep in mind the most important deciding factor is what is God saying? He won't ask you or me to go into a situation or a relationship He knows we are not ready to handle. But, at the same time, it may be He knows you are ready to handle the situation and is sending you because of your background.

The key is seeking the Holy Spirit's leading and then staying focused on Jesus in each situation.

The final place Jesus challenges us to go is "the ends of the earth". The word "ends" comes from the Greek word eschatos (Strong's Greek – 2078). It means the last in time or place, or rank, the worst. As I looked at the Strong's list of definitions, I was struck by the "last in place or rank". The question that flashed in my mind was, "Where is the last place I want to go to share Jesus?" Right behind it, "Who is the last person on Earth with whom I want to share Jesus?" And, I have to admit, that really struck home.

Think about it for a moment. Is there someone with whom you never wish to speak to again, let alone share the news about how they can share Heaven with you? Is there a person you pray to never see because, if you do, you would need to ask their forgiveness? Or worse, you may need to forgive? Is there a place where "outside your comfort zone" doesn't even begin to describe the fear, the horror you feel when you think about it?

These places, these people are real. The hurt you experienced, the destruction of your soul, the emotions inflicted on you is indescribable. No words exist that can describe what happens inside of you on a regular basis when their name pops up. In this view of the verse, these are "the ends of the Earth". And Jesus calls us to go there.

I don't say this lightly. Yes, I have been hurt by people in my life, but I don't dare assume I have suffered as deeply as you may have. I'm not here to tell you how helpful it will be when you take this step. I am not qualified to suggest that sharing Jesus with this person will make it better. And, I don't even begin to think I know if or when you should take this step. Only Jesus knows. Only His Spirit can lead you there. Only His presence and His love can sustain you through that valley.

What I can share is this. Jesus did it for you and for me. He suffered excruciating pain and death so that I could be reconciled to God. He does not ask us to do more than He did. The more I learned about crucifixion, the more I realized this. And, I know that Jesus will ask me to be an example of Him in places I will not want to go and with people I do not want to see. In this sense, He is asking me to be His *martrus,* a martyr. He asks me to die to myself, to the anger I feel, to the pain I carry so that He can live in me.

He is patient with me, and with you. He knows us better than we know ourselves. He will never force us to go there. That is a part of the free will He has given us. But, I also have to believe He will not take me there unless it is for my own good, my own growth. The journey will probably hurt; the Cross did. But Jesus knows what is on the other side. He knows the darkness of that valley will be overcome by the beauty at the other end. It may not be a quick journey and it may be a long time before we ever understand what Jesus knew when He asked us to go there.

As I look again at Acts 1:8, it becomes more than a Sunday standard call to overseas mission's involvement or getting involved in a community outreach program. Now, it goes from abstract to painfully personal. It forces me to examine myself and my relationships, especially painful relationships. It challenges me to once again see to what level I have allowed the love and healing of Jesus to penetrate into my heart. It asks me if I am ready to open a part of myself that, till now, I have been reluctant to turn over to the Holy Spirit.

I guess this is what Paul means when He says, "So then, dear friends, just you have always obeyed, not only in my presence, but even more in my absence, continue working out your salvation with awe and reverence[14]". In the original Greek, the word "awe" is *phobos* (Strong's Greek – 5401) or exceeding fear or terror. And, in going to the ends of the earth, I will be terrified.

In Jerusalem, there probably won't be any fear. It's a good place to practice. In Judea, there's a bit of nervousness, but there still seems to be a relative sense of emotional security. Here I can begin to stretch myself, to grow my trust in

---

[14] Phil. 2.12 NET

God's love. As I move into Samaria, I begin to expose the gaps between what I say I believe and what I actually do. And, the ends of the Earth? It is here that Jesus is calling me to take up my cross and follow Him. The further I move from Jerusalem, my comfort zone, the greater I find myself having to die to myself, my thoughts, my feelings, my own emotions. And, it is in when I am faced with dying to myself I learn how much further I still have to go in closing the gap between what I say I believe and what my actions say about what I believe.

The First Belief Choice

"Did God really say,..."[15] is the first instance where Man had to choose to believe God or believe someone else. Genesis is barely 2 chapters old. God has presented the Garden of Eden open for use by Adam (Eve is still waiting to make her entrance). There was one restriction- when he eats of the Tree of Knowledge of Good and Evil, he will die[16]. It's pretty clear cut – eat and die. It doesn't say when he would die, just that they would die.

Fast forward to chapter 3. Eve is now on the scene as Adam's helpmate. He has let her know the simple rule of the Garden – don't eat the fruit from the tree of the knowledge of good and evil. That's it. Every other tree provides fruit that is good to eat. Just not that one.

---

[15] Gen 3:1b New Living Translation
[16] Gen 2:17 NLT

One day, Adam and Eve are near the tree. A crafty serpent strikes up a conversation with Eve[17]. The word used to describe the serpent, "shrewdest", is important. The original Hebrew word is `aruwm (Hebrew Strong's 6175). `Aruwm can mean subtle (used in the King Jams version), shrewd, sly, sensible, prudent or crafty. In other words, the conversation the serpent is starting with Eve is not an innocent one. The serpent is not asking because he does not know. He knows; the question is simply a way to plant the first seed of doubt into Eve's mind.

To begin with, he asks a question, which he knows, is incorrectly phrased. "Did God really say, 'You must not eat from *any* tree in the Garden'?" (*italics* mine). The serpent knew what God had said. Remember, he is shrewd, crafty. Eve's response gets closer to the original rule, but swings to the other end of the pendulum and adds her (or Adam's) own restriction to it.

---

[17] Gen 3:1 NLT

"Oh no, we can eat fruit from the trees in the Garden. It's only the one in the middle we can't eat from. In fact, we can't even <u>touch</u> it[18]." (Underline mine).

Now, I don't know where Eve got the extra prohibition of touching the tree. Maybe Adam passed it on that way in order to impress upon her the danger of the tree's fruit. Maybe it was how Eve heard what Adam had said. Maybe she felt if she added that bit, it would help her keep the only rule they had. Regardless of why it was there, here is the first instance of God's law (and there was only one law) being amended by man.

As a side note, it's pretty well known that Eve was not alone. Verse 6 of chapter 3 says her husband was with her. And I don't know why the serpent didn't approach him, why he wasn't involved in the conversation, why he didn't notice or say anything when Eve picked the

---

[18] Gen 3:2

forbidden fruit, or eat it. All sorts of reasons, guesses, conjectures and opinions have been offered. Scholars have blamed Eve for being weak in listening to the serpent. They have chastised Adam for being weak for not stepping in and protecting his wife. The fact is both were weak. To blame one more than the other seems to be counterproductive. Sin is sin and they both sinned.

Eve's sin – she looked at the tree through the lenses of the serpent's words, "You won't die. God knows your eyes will be opened as soon as you eat it and you will be like God, knowing both good and evil[19]" She allowed her mind to be a fertile ground for the seed of doubt. She looked at the fruit in a new light. There were now two different ways to look at the fruit. There was the choice of who to believe. She could choose to see it through God's eyes – eating it will bring death. She could choose to believe the serpent's take on the fruit – you

---

[19] Gen 3:5 NLT

won't die; you'll become like God. She chose the serpent's point of view –she looked at the tree, saw it was good (in her own definition of the word) for food, and she wanted wisdom[20]. So, she took a piece and ate it.

Adam's sin - he also had the choice of who to believe – God or the serpent. Yes, it was Eve that gave it to him, but he was there, in front of the tree, by his wife, aware of what was happening. He could have stepped in to save her; he didn't. He could have chosen not to eat the fruit when Eve passed it to him. He didn't. He had no excuse. We don't know definitively why he, or Eve, chose to believe the serpent over God, but they did.

As I said, this isn't about who holds the greatest responsibility for the Fall. In God's eyes, all three were equally guilty. Each was cursed, each was punished. What is important is to back up and look at is the way the serpent introduced

---

[20] Gen 3:6 NLT

the sinful choice. "Did God really say...?" That phrase echoes again and again in our brains. It shows up in something as simple as a speed limit, as complex as a tax return, as dangerous as an improper relationship. "Did God really say" tempts you, it tempts me every day. Was God really thinking about pesky things like speed limits when He said, "Everyone must submit to the governing authorities, for all authority comes from God, and those in positions of authority have been placed there by God."[21] I'm a safe driver. My car can handle these speeds. I'm late. No one is around.

Surely, Jesus wasn't thinking about my taxes today when He responded to the Pharisees' question 2,000 years ago, "Give to Caesar what is Caesar's, and to God what is God's.[22]" But God, my tax money is used for things I don't think You approve of. Do I really have to include that cash I got for that simple job? Things are

---

[21] Rom 13:1 NLT
[22] Matt. 22:21 NLT

tight, God. I need the money to pay bills 'cause unlike the government, I get in trouble if I don't pay my bills. All of these are a variation of, "Did God really say...?"

Did God really say that sex was only for a man and a woman who were married...to each other? Leviticus 18 goes to great lengths to answer this question. Proverbs is full of warnings against looking outside the marriage bed. Paul warns the Romans, the Ephesians, and the Colossians about sexual sin.

It seems in today's church there is a sin scale. It can range from "shame on you" to "you're damned to Hell" depending on what you do. If it is something a majority of us do, like gluttony or gossip, nothing is said. We stay silent to protect us all. We look the other way at an engaged couple is living together before being married because it is, well, what is done. On the other hand, we will vehemently condemn a homosexual with the same fury of the mob that dragged the woman caught in adultery before

Jesus.[23] Surely, God, You can't mean that all
sins are equally wrong? Galatians 5:19-21 says,
"Yes".

And it isn't that we ask the qualifying question
of the same sins. Some of us know and obey all
God's commands for sexual purity without
hesitation yet over Indulge in gossip. Others are
gracious in speech yet unable to control
gluttony. We pass off prejudice as discernment.
We say we can't serve in church because it cuts
into family time. We find all sorts of
justifications that begin with, "Did God really
say...?"

The biggest problem isn't that we are unaware
of God's commands. The problem is the length
we go to put our sin into an acceptable light; it
is really of question of challenging God's
commands, of trying to minimize our
disobedience. Or, it could be adding to God's
commands things He didn't. Eve added to God's

---

[23] John 8:3

command that they couldn't even touch the tree. Whether it was proper or not for her to create a bigger buffer zone against sin, it didn't work. The first time we're told she was challenged with, "Did God really say...?" both she and Adam chose to believe the serpent over God.

For me, the kicker is the serpent presented something God later encourages us to seek – wisdom. "Your eyes will be opened." "When the woman saw the fruit was beautiful...and she wanted the wisdom it would give her...[24]" Hey, aren't we supposed to seek wisdom? Isn't Proverbs full of such commands? Weren't Adam and Eve only trying to pursue something God wanted for them?

It wasn't wisdom that the serpent was offering. If Adam or Eve had been paying attention, they would have heard the serpent tempting them with be like "...you will be like God, knowing

---

[24] Gen 3.6

both good and evil."[25] Compare that wording to the passage that describe' s Lucifer's, "I will climb to the highest mountains; and *be like the Most High*.[26]" (*italics* mine). Now, Adam and Eve didn't have Isaiah's insights back then, but we do. And this is the whole "What's wrong with it" about the phrase, "Did God really say…?" There are appropriate times to ask this question. We can ask that question if we are <u>truly</u> seeking God's commands. There are gems in His word He uncovers. I remember the first time I caught this phrase, "He was testing Philip for He already knew what He was going to do[27]." I can genuinely ask, "Did God really say that…?" because I had never seen it that way.

Where I wander into the sin zone is when I ask that question to try and find wiggle room for "reinterpreting" His commands. Did God really say thirds and fourths at dinner was wrong? Did God really say that gossiping with others about

---

[25] Gen 3:5b
[26] Isa 14.14
[27] John 6:

my neighbor's affair was sin? Is it true that just because we don't know something is sin doesn't make it OK? Yes! This is why we are regularly encouraged study His Word, to gain His wisdom and to share with others. Ignorance of right and wrong is not excused.

How about you? Do you know what God commands? Do you study His Word to learn what He expects of you? Are the boundaries you set for yourself in line with Scripture? Are they less than God sets up? Are they stricter than God set up? Do you know why you have the boundaries you do?

These are important questions. As we grow in our relationship with God, we need to be able to answer the question "Did God really say…" for things we're not sure about. We need to ask this question about things we think we are sure about. And for those sins we do know are sin, we must respond when the serpent tempts us with, "Did God really say…" by responding, "Yes, He really did."

Made in the USA
San Bernardino, CA
10 February 2016